SPAGHETTI *Madness*

First published in 2019
ISBN: 978-0-6485614-6-0
Published by Louie Loves Food Publishing

Cover image by iStock
Design by Green Hill Publishing
Photographs by Louie Laudonia and iStock
Clock by Anhar Ismail from the Noun Project
People by Ragal Kartidev from the Noun Project

By Louie Laudonia

Inspired by Great Food

Rose, Calabria,
1995

Where it all began...

Welcome to Spaghetti Madness!

My interest in cooking started when I was a little kid growing up in the north eastern suburbs in Adelaide, South Australia. Coming from a southern Italian background, meant we never went hungry. I vividly remember in primary school and at lunch time pulling out of my lunch box this huge Panini stuffed with last night's leftovers, I felt like a magician pulling a rabbit out of his hat. Whether it was stuffed eggplant, schnitzel or homemade salami, I was always full at school and I hardly got a simple lunch of vegemite or ham sandwiches. Though, I did swap one of my sandwiches for a vegemite sandwich…I was hooked.

My mum and dad have always had chickens and a veggie garden, growing the freshest and organically grown produce which meant family traditions were abundant. And at different times of the year and without skipping a heartbeat we were making tomato sauce, sausage making, wine making, sometimes making olive oil and sometimes baking breads.

Naturally I started cooking at an early age, helping mum in the kitchen. But my true love of good food started back in 1995 when visiting my nonni's in Calabria in a little village called Rose. There I started working in a restaurant called 'Il Mulino'. Owned by Umberto and Teresa Castiglione, they took me under their wings and showed me what rustic Calabrian food was all about, I loved it! It showed be a way of going back to basics and appreciating great food in its simplistic form.

It has been a long journey for me to get to this stage of having confidence to share my views and recipes of fantastic food from around the world and fulfilling a dream of publishing my first cook book, hope you like it.

Much love,

Louie Landonia

Contents

Spaghetti

Spaghetti with Meatballs

 **Prep Time 30 mins | Cook Time 60 mins**    4-6 people

Learn how to make meatballs for spaghetti and even get the kids involved with this very easy homemade meatball recipe. Served over a bed of spaghetti with hearty marinara sauce, this pasta favourite is guaranteed to please the entire family.

INGREDIENTS FOR THE SAUCE

¼ cup extra virgin olive oil.

1 medium onion, chopped (about 1 cup).

5 x 400g cans plum or roma tomatoes with their liquid.

½ teaspoon red chilli flakes.

3 dried bay leaves.

Salt and pepper to taste.

INGREDIENTS FOR THE MEATBALLS

500g minced beef.

1 cup dry breadcrumbs, finely crumbled.

1 cup freshly grated parmesan cheese.

¼ cup chopped fresh Italian parsley.

2 cloves of garlic, minced.

1 teaspoon of salt

¼ teaspoon of pepper.

1 large egg, beaten.

All-purpose flour for dredging.

ADDITIONAL INGREDIENTS

¼ cup of olive oil.

¼ cup vegetable oil.

500g spaghetti (or your favourite pasta).

1. To prepare the sauce, heat ¼ cup of olive oil in a heavy bottomed pot **over** medium heat. Add onion and sauté for about 4 minutes.

2. Pour in tomatoes (with their liquid), along with the chilli flakes, bay leaves. Stir together. Bring to barely a simmer and using a potato masher or fork mash the heck out of the tomatoes. Stir and add salt and pepper to taste.

3. Bring to a full simmer and let it cook for about 30 minutes, stirring occasionally. Taste and adjust seasonings to your preference. Continue to cook over low heat.

4. To prepare the meatballs, loosely crumble the beef into a large bowl. Sprinkle the breadcrumbs, ⅓ of a cup of grated parmesan, chopped parsley, garlic, salt and pepper over the beef. Add the beaten egg and using clean hands, GENTLY combine ingredients. Try not to mash the ingredients together. I think the meatball mixture is better when they are not mashed to death. Shape into 4cm meatballs.

5. Lightly dredge the meatballs in the flour until evenly coated and place on a baking tray or plate. In a heavy skillet over medium to high, heat ¼ cup vegetable oil.

6. Cooking in batches, add meatballs into the skillet without crowding. Fry each batch for about 6 minutes, turning to brown all sides of each meatball. Adjust heat to prevent over-browning. Place browned meatballs on paper towel lined surface.

7. Once all meatballs are browned, add to prepared sauce, gently stirring to coat meatballs with sauce. Continue to cook for about 30 minutes until meatballs are cooked through (no pink remaining in centre).

8. Cook spaghetti or your preferred pasta according to package directions. Drain pasta and serve topped with sauce and meatballs. Garnish with grated parmesan cheese.

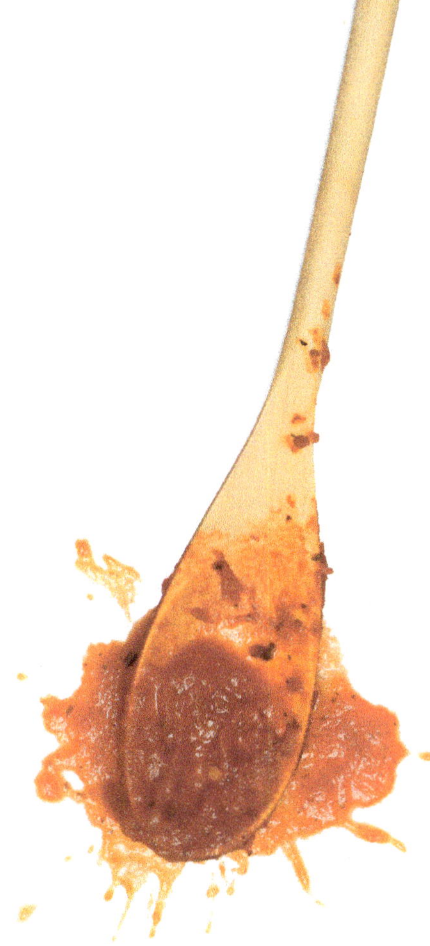

# Spaghetti Puttanesca

Spaghetti Puttanesca, invented in Naples in the mid-20th century is a fantastic dish packed with an aromatic punch. This classic dish has a spicy sauce made from tomatoes, chilli flakes, capers, anchovies, olives, garlic and fresh herbs. For a dish so simple, you would be hard pressed to find one so flavourfully complex.

INGREDIENTS

500g spaghetti.

2 tablespoons olive oil.

4-6 anchovies fillets packed in oil, chopped.

3-4 garlic cloves, minced.

½ handful of fresh basil leaves, chopped.

1 tablespoon of small capers.

1 x 400g can diced tomatoes.

⅓ cup black olives, pitted.

Freshly grated parmesan or pecorino cheese.

METHOD

1. Set a large pot filled with water on the stove and bring to boil, add salt and spaghetti. Set the timer according to package directions. Meanwhile, sauté chopped anchovies in olive oil over low heat while stirring and breaking them up with a wooden spoon for 1-2 minutes. They will start to turn into a paste, add garlic and continue stirring for 1 minute.

2. Add tomatoes, chopped basil, capers and olives, turn the heat up and bring the sauce to a boil, lower the heat to low and simmer for 6-7 more minutes.

3. Stir occasionally and try break up big tomato chunks with the wooden spoon. Drain spaghetti and add to the pan with the sauce. Toss gently and serve with freshly grated parmesan or pecorino cheese.

Spaghetti Carbonara

 **Prep Time 10 mins | Cook Time 20 mins**  4-5 people

With just a few quality ingredients, this classic creamy carbonara is simple, elegant and guaranteed to make your eyes roll back in pure bliss with every bite. Creamy carbonara is made using just eggs, pecorino romano cheese, cured pork and pepper.

INGREDIENTS

500g spaghetti.

200g pancetta or bacon, diced.

1 large garlic clove, skin intact and smashed.

4 large eggs.

75g pecorino romano cheese, freshly grated.

1 teaspoon black pepper.

METHOD

1. Bring a large pot of water to boil. Add pasta and cook according to package directions. Do not drain the water as it is needed later.

2. In a small bowl, whisk together the eggs and ¾ of the grated pecorino cheese. Place the pancetta or bacon and garlic clove in a large skillet. Turn heat to medium and cook, stirring every minute, until the pancetta or bacon has browned, but not crisp, about 5-7 minutes. Remove and discard the garlic, then add the black pepper.

3. Reserving about half a cup of the pasta water, drain the spaghetti and add it to the pancetta or bacon. Toss until the spaghetti is coated with the pancetta fat. Remove from heat and add about a ⅓ cup of the pasta water.

4. While stirring and tossing the pasta, pour in the eggs, continuing to toss until the spaghetti is well coated and glossy. Add additional pasta water if necessary, to get a creamy consistency. To serve, use tongs to pick up a good serving of pasta. Place the tongs on a large spoon and twist to wrap them in the spaghetti. Place the spaghetti on a plate while twisting and slowly release the tongs, leaving a serving that resembles a bird's nest. Sprinkle with additional pecorino romano cheese and cracked black pepper.

Spaghetti with Italian Sausage & Vodka Sauce

 **Prep Time 10 mins | Cook Time 30 mins**    7-8 people

Spaghetti with Italian sausage in a creamy, meaty and tasty VODKA sauce. The sauce with hearty chunks of sausage and a good splash of vodka and tossed through al dente pasta it's guaranteed to be a new family favourite to make this perfect for those busy weeknight dinners.

Vodka sauce is a pasta sauce made from San Marzano crushed tomatoes, heavy cream, vodka and Italian herbs. The alcohol in the vodka acts as an emulsifier which keeps the acidity of the tomatoes from separating the cream as well as enhances the flavour of the tomatoes creating a more intense taste.

INGREDIENTS

500g spaghetti.

1 tablespoon olive oil.

1 tablespoon butter.

1 medium sweet onion, peeled and finely chopped.

3 garlic cloves, peeled and minced.

500g hot Italian sausage, casings removed and crumbled.

1 cup of vodka.

1 cup of chicken stock.

2 x 400g cans of San Marzano crushed tomatoes.

Salt and pepper to taste

1 cup of heavy or thickened cream.

Basil leaves, chopped.

Fresh parmesan cheese.

METHOD

1. In a pot over medium heat, bring the salted water to a boil. Add spaghetti, cook according to package directions, around 8-10 minutes and drain well in a colander. In a pot over medium heat, add olive oil and butter. Heat until butter begins to melt.

2. Add onions and cook, stirring occasionally, for about 3-5 minutes or until softened and begins to slightly caramelize. Add garlic and cook for about 30 to 40 seconds or until aromatic. Add Italian sausage and cook, breaking into pieces with back of the spoon, until lightly browned. Drain excess fast as needed.

3. Add vodka and cook for about 2-4 minutes or until reduced by half. Add chicken stock and crushed tomatoes. Bring to a boil. Lower heat and simmer, stirring occasionally, for about 8-10 minutes or until meat is fully cooked and sauce is reduced. Season with salt and pepper to taste.

4. Add the cream and stir to combine. Continue to simmer for about 3-5 minutes or until sauce begins to bubble. Remove from heat.

5. Divide spaghetti onto serving plates, ladle sauce on top, garnish with basil leaves and sprinkle with shaved parmesan cheese if desired.

Baked Million Dollar Spaghetti

 **Prep Time 30 mins | Cook Time 40 mins**    9-10 people

My family adores this baked spaghetti casserole as it is the ultimate comfort food for those cold nights. This dish is a family favourite that's filled with pasta, cheese and an easy spaghetti meat sauce. Even for those fussy eaters this will disappear very quickly. Serve with a salad and garlic bread for a delicious hearty family dinner.

INGREDIENTS

500g spaghetti,
  cooked 2 minutes shy of directions and drained.
500g minced beef.
1 medium onion, chopped finely.
2 garlic cloves, minced.
Salt and pepper to taste.
6 cups of ready-made marinara sauce
225g cream cheese, softened.
3 cups of shredded mozzarella cheese.
Parsley, chopped (optional as a garnish)

METHOD

1. Preheat oven to 180 degrees Celsius. In a large skillet add the minced beef, onions, garlic, salt and pepper into the pan and cook on high. Once browned, turn off the heat, drain the liquid left in pan and mix in one cup of marinara sauce. In a bowl add the cooked spaghetti to the remaining 5 cups of the marinara sauce and toss to combine. Then mix the cream cheese and 2 cups of mozzarella cheese in another bowl.

2. Add half the pasta/sauce to the bottom of a 30cm x 20cm pan. Add the cream cheese mixture and top with the remaining pasta/sauce mixture. Add the meat sauce mixture on top of the pasta and top with remaining cup of mozzarella cheese.

3. Cover and bake for 30 minutes, then uncover and bake for an additional 10 minutes, until the cheese is slightly golden, melted and bubbly. Serve with crusty garlic bread and salad….or just on it's own.

Buon appetito!

Spaghetti with Basil Pesto

 **Prep Time 15 mins | Cook Time 10 mins**    4-5 people

When preparing this recipe, like most recipes, you'll want to use the freshest ingredients you can find. I always argue that fresh is best especially when a recipe has very few ingredients. You really do want the flavours to be bright and present. Just add a few dollops of basil pesto to your favourite cooked pasta- it doesn't have to be spaghetti at all! This is a dinner fit for royalty, or at least your family and preferred friends.

INGREDIENTS

1 large bunch of fresh basil

2 garlic cloves, smashed and peeled.

¼ cup pine nuts, lightly toasted.

½ cup extra virgin olive oil.

1 cup freshly grated pecorino romano cheese.

½ teaspoon salt, plus more for seasoning.

Freshly ground black pepper.

500g spaghetti.

1 /2 teaspoon red chilli flakes.

1 tablespoon of scallions, chopped for garnish if desired.

METHOD

1. Pluck large basil leaves from stems, the smaller ones are ok and you should have about 2 cups of leaves. Wash the basil leaves in a large bowl of cold water and dry in a salad spinner or pat dry with paper towels.

2. Put the basil, garlic and pine nuts in a food processor and pulse until coarsely chopped. With the processor running, gradually add the olive oil and process until the pesto is smooth. Transfer the pesto to a large bowl and stir in ½ cup of the cheese. Season with salt and pepper.

3. Bring a large pot of cold water to a boil over high heat and salt it generously. Add the pasta and boil, stirring occasionally and cook to package directions. Drain into a colander but save ¼ cup of the pasta water. Add the pasta to the bowl. Use tongs and toss with enough of the cooking water so the pesto coats the pasta evenly. Season with salt and pepper to taste, plate up, sprinkle with grated cheese and a little chilli if desired. Serve warm.

and buon appetito.

Spaghetti with Seafood

 **Prep Time 10 mins | Cook Time 20 mins**    4 people

---

The ultimate spaghetti Frutti di Mare! A very popular Italian pasta dish meaning "fruit of the sea" made with the freshest seafood you can get your hands on. Consisting of prawns, clams, squid and mussels tossed through an arrabiata sauce…why go out when this can be enjoyed at home. Buon appetito.

INGREDIENTS

250g clams, cleaned well.

250g mussels, debearded and cleaned well.

500g prawns, peeled and deveined.

250g squid, tentacles and tubes cut into small pieces.

¼ cup extra virgin olive oil.

4 garlic cloves, minced.

1 teaspoon of red chilli flakes, plus extra to taste.

½ cup white wine.

⅓ cup fresh Italian parsley, chopped.

1 batch of arrabiata tomato sauce,
   made in advance or store bought.

Sea salt to taste.

METHOD

1. Bring a large pot of salted water to a boil. Cook the spaghetti according to package directions until al dente. Drain and reserve 1 cup of the salty pasta water.

2. Meanwhile heat up your largest skillet on low to medium flame. Add a little olive oil, the garlic and red chilli flakes. Stir quickly making sure not to burn the garlic. Add the clams and mussels and toss them around. Pour in the white wine and cover with a lid. Cook for about a minute or so until the clams and mussels start to open, discard any that remain closed. Add the prawns to the skillet and give it a stir. Cover and cook for another minute or so.

3. Once all the clams and mussels have opened and the prawns are almost cooked add the squid and cook for another 30 seconds or so until they curl up. Taste for seasonings and add more sea salt if needed. Remember that shellfish will spit out a lot of sea water during cooking, so wait til the end to season.

4. Meanwhile warm up the sauce in a saucepan. Pour the sauce over the seafood and toss to coat well. Add the cooked spaghetti to the skillet with the seafood and toss to coat in the sauce. Add a little bit of the reserved pasta water if needed to stretch out the sauce. Transfer your seafood spaghetti to a serving platter, drizzle with a little olive oil and sprinkle with chopped parsley.

Spaghetti with Breadcrumbs and Anchovies

 **Prep Time 20 mins | Cook Time 20 mins**    7-8 people

---

There is something very Sicilian about this dish, even though it was a dish my family from Calabria used to cook up during Christmas time. Toasted breadcrumbs were used to be a cheap substitute for emulating the flavour and texture of grated cheese when times were tough. These days having a canister filled with toasted breadcrumbs is surprisingly decadent.

INGREDIENTS

2 cups toasted breadcrumbs,
  homemade very much preferred.
¾ cup extra virgin olive oil, divided into ½ cup and ¼ cup.
500g spaghetti
4 garlic cloves, minced.
50g anchovies and their oil, or to taste.
1 teaspoon cracked black pepper, or to taste.
2 teaspoons red chilli flakes, or to taste.
¾ cup walnuts, chopped.
½ cup sultanas.
½ cup parsley, chopped finely.

METHOD

1. Take some stale bread and grind it in a food processor until you have 2 cups of course breadcrumbs. Next, in a skillet, heat ½ cup of olive oil over medium to low heat. Add the bread crumbs, stir to combine. Let them toast lightly, watching them carefully. They should get quite darkly toasted, you want them to be crunchy. Remove from the heat and set aside.

2. Boil the pasta in salted water as per package directions until al dente. While that is happening, heat another ¼ cup of olive oil over medium to high heat. Add the minced garlic and let it caramelize. Next, add the anchovies with their oil and use a wooden spoon to break them up until you have something that resembles a coarse paste.

3. Next add the walnuts, chilli flakes, sultanas, parsley and black pepper and stir through. Now add the cooked pasta and quickly toss in the breadcrumbs. Plate up immediately with a little sprinkling of toasted breadcrumbs on top…I hope you enjoy this favourite of mine.

Buon appetito.

18   SPAGHETTI MADNESS

Spaghetti Bolognese

 **Prep Time 30 mins | Cook Time 90 mins**    4 people

---

A true Italian classic!
For a quick midweek dinner or a slow cooked weekend indulgence, this Bolognese sauce is rich, thick and has a delicious depth of flavour. It is super easy and can be made in advance and frozen in portions for those times that a quick meal for the family is needed…buon appetito.

INGREDIENTS

2 tablespoon olive oil.

6 rashers smoked streaky pancetta or bacon, chopped.

2 medium onions, finely chopped.

2 carrots, trimmed and finely chopped.

2 celery sticks, finely chopped.

3 garlic cloves, minced.

2 x 400g cans of plum or roma tomatoes, diced.

A small amount of fresh basil, leaves picked, ¾ finely
    chopped and the rest left for garnish

1 teaspoon dried oregano.

2 bay leaves.

1 red chilli, deseeded and finely chopped (optional).

250ml red wine.

800g lean minced beef.

800g spaghetti.

TO SEASON AND SERVE

100g parmesan cheese, freshly grated, plus extra to serve.

Crusty bread, to serve (optional).

METHOD

1. Heat the oil in a large, heavy based saucepan and fry the bacon until golden over a medium heat. Add the onions, carrots, celery and continue stirring. Add the garlic and fry until softened and aromatic. Increase heat and add the minced beef and cook until it has browned.

2. Pour in the wine and boil until it has reduced in volume by about a third. Reduce the heat and stir in the tomatoes. Cover with lid and simmer over a gentle heat for 1-1 ½ hours, stirring occasionally, until it's rich and thickened.

3. Cook the pasta in plenty of boiling salted water. Drain and divide between plates. Sprinkle a little parmesan over the pasta before adding a good ladleful of the sauce. Finish with a good sprinkling of cheese and a twist of black pepper. Buon appetito.

4. Any leftover sauce, once cooled can be poured into zip lock bags or a container to freeze to quickly thaw out later for a quick weeknight dinner.

Spaghetti alle Vongole

 **Prep Time 2 hrs | Cook Time 18 mins**    4 people

Vongole also known as cockles, pipis, surf clams and baby clams. Regardless of what they are called they are the heroes of this exquisite dish. A dish so simple in ingredients, but if you want to make this I stress to you 'only the freshest of ingredients' and you will have something that will make your mouth water.

INGREDIENTS

800g vongole

8 tablespoon extra-virgin olive oil.

7 garlic cloves, minced.

1 teaspoon red chilli flakes.

200g tomatoes, chopped.

150ml dry white wine.

Pinch of brown sugar.

400g spaghetti.

15g butter.

15g flat-leaf parsley.

METHOD

1. To clean the vongole, soak for 2 hours in cool, salted water, first discarding any that have cracked shells or do not close after being tapped on the side of the bowl. Drain and rinse well under cold running water.

2. Put 6 tablespoons of olive oil, garlic and chilli flakes in a pan over medium heat. As soon as the garlic sizzles without browning, stir and quickly add the chopped tomatoes followed by the wine. Turn up the heat and cook for around 3-4 minutes.

3. Add the vongole, stir and cover with a tight lid and cook for a further 4 minutes, shaking occasionally until all the vongole are open. Add the sugar, season and cook for another 2 minutes and discard any that have not opened.

4. Cook the spaghetti in a large pan of boiling salted water according to package directions, drain and return to the pan with the butter. Add the vongole mixture and most of the parsley. Shake the pan and serve immediately, scattered with the rest of the parsley and olive oil.

Creamy Lemon Spaghetti with Salmon

 **Prep Time 15 mins | Cook Time 15 mins**    4 people

---

Need to impress, this is it! A dish that is on the table in 20 minutes flat. Pan fried flakey salmon and spaghetti served in a light lemon cream sauce.

INGREDIENTS

400g spaghetti.

1 tablespoon extra virgin olive oil.

1 teaspoon butter.

Pinch of salt and pepper.

3 boneless salmon fillets.

1 small onion, peeled and chopped.

2 garlic cloves, minced.

2 tablespoon white wine.

5 tablespoon double/heavy cream.

Zest of 1 lemon.

1 small zucchini, cut into thin strips.

Juice of half lemon.

TO SEASON AND SERVE

2 tablespoon freshly grated parmesan
  or grana padano cheese.

Pinch of black pepper.

Lemon zest.

METHOD

1. Place the spaghetti in a large pot of boiling salted water and simmer according to package directions. Whilst the spaghetti is cooking, heat oil and butter in a large frying pan. Sprinkle a pinch of salt and pepper on the salmon fillets and place in the frying pan skin side down. Cook for 3 minutes, until the skin is crispy. Turn the salmon over and add the onions to the pan.

2. Cook the salmon and onions for a further 3 minutes, until the onions start to soften. Take the salmon out of the pan and place on a chopping board. Add the garlic to the onions and cook for a minute whilst stirring. Add the wine and let it bubble for a minute, then add the cream. Heat slowly.

3. While the cream is heating through, remove the skin from salmon and break into rough chunks. Now add the salmon back into the pan with the cream. And now add the lemon zest.

4. By now the spaghetti is almost ready, add the sugar and thin strips of zucchini with the spaghetti for the last minute of cooking.

5. Drain the pasta, reserving about half a cup of the pasta water. Add the spaghetti and the strips of zucchini to the frying pan and toss through along with a good splash of the pasta water and the lemon juice. Divide between 4 bowls and top with freshly grated parmesan, freshly ground black pepper and a little bit of lemon zest.

Buon appetito.

Classic Cacio e Pepe

You may have seen kitchen staff in an Italian restaurant bringing out a cart with a huge wheel of Pecorino Romano cheese with a slight cavity on top to your table, twirling freshly cooked spaghetti in it, then plating it up with a generous amount of cracked black pepper over the top of the pasta. That ladies and gentlemen is 'Cacio e Pepe…this is heaven on a plate! A classic dish from Rome where it originated centuries ago. 'Cacio e Pepe' is perfectly delicious in its incredible simplicity…pasta, Pecorino Romano cheese and freshly cracked black pepper. The name literally means cheese and pepper. Just a few high quality ingredients and technique is all that is needed to master this dish that you'll never forget. Buon appetito.

INGREDIENTS

400g spaghetti

4 tablespoons butter, divided.

1 tablespoon extra virgin olive oil.

Coarsely cracked black pepper.

1 ¼ cup freshly grated pecorino romano cheese.

1 ¼ cup freshly grated parmesan cheese,
  plus more for garnish.

METHOD

1. In a pot of boiling salted water, cook pasta according to package directions, until al dente. Reserve 2/3 cup of pasta water and drain pasta.

2. In a large skillet over medium heat, melt 2 tablespoons of butter with oil. Add a generous amount of freshly cracked black pepper and toast until fragrant, about 1 minute.

3. Add ⅓ cup reserved pasta water and bring to a simmer. Whisk in remaining butter then, using tongs toss pasta into butter mixture.

4. Add the cheeses and toss constantly until cheese is melty, removing skillet from heat when about half the cheese has melted. If the sauce is too thick, loosen with more pasta water. Serve immediately.

Spaghetti Salad

 **Prep Time 20 mins | Cook Time 8 mins**    15 people

---

This is a great cold summer salad, so easy and quick to make. Perfect for when entertaining. With beautiful colours, delicious flavours and crisp textures this will surely be a hit with everyone. Buon appetito.

INGREDIENTS

500 g spaghetti, broke into 3-4 pieces.

3 Roma tomatoes, diced.

1 medium zucchini, diced.

1 red capsicum, diced.

1 green capsicum, diced.

1 cucumber, diced.

1 red onion, diced.

120 g sliced olives, drained.

225 g cheddar cheese or something equivalent, cut into small cubes.

DRESSING

350ml of Italian dressing.

¼ cup grated parmesan cheese.

1 teaspoon paprika.

¼ teaspoon garlic powder.

METHOD

1. In a pot of boiling salted water add spaghetti and cook according to package directions, then rinse in cold water and drain. Set aside and let cool, just toss a little olive oil through it so it won't stick together.

2. Place tomatoes, zucchini, capsicum, onion, cucumber, olives and cheese in a large bowl. Add cooled spaghetti and mix well.

3. In a small bowl, mix together dressing, parmesan cheese, paprika, garlic powder. Pour on top of the spaghetti and vegetables and mix until completely combined.

4. Let it sit in the fridge for at least 2 hours before serving as this salad gets better with time as the flavours meld together.

# Four Cheese Spaghetti

Do you want a side of spaghetti with your cheese? If cheese is one of your main food groups then this velvety smooth dish is for you, perfect for a week night dinner ready in 20 minutes flat.

INGREDIENTS

400g spaghetti.

1 tablespoon extra virgin olive oil.

3 garlic cloves, minced.

¾ cup cream cheese, softened.

¼ cup romano cheese, grated.

¼ cup mozzarella cheese, grated.

¼ cup parmesan cheese, grated.

¾ cup chicken broth or stock.

Salt and freshly ground black pepper.

2 tablespoons of chives, chopped for garnish.

METHOD

1. In a large pot of boiling salted water, cook pasta according to package directions, until al dente. Meanwhile, in a large skillet over medium heat, heat oil. Add garlic and cook until it's aromatic, about 1 minute. Now add the softened cream cheese, chicken broth and ½ cup of reserved pasta water.

2. Add cooked spaghetti and toss until they are fully coated and liquid is simmering.

3. Remove from heat and stir in the cheeses. Toss constantly, adding more pasta water until sauce reaches desired consistency. Season with salt and pepper and garnish with chives before serving,

Spaghetti and Meatball Cups

Spaghetti is probably one of those busy week night go-to dinner ideas. Super-fast, boil the pasta, warm up the sauce, toss together and serve. Everyone loves spaghetti and if you have extra time you can take it one step further and create these delicious spaghetti and meatball cups. Perfect for the kids or when entertaining.

INGREDIENTS

400g spaghetti.

3 large eggs, divided.

1 and ½ cups shredded mozzarella.

¾ cup grated parmesan cheese, divided,
   plus more for garnish.

3 cups marinara sauce, divided.

Cooking spray, for pan.

500g minced beef.

½ cup bread crumbs.

2 garlic cloves, minced.

2 tablespoon fresh flat leaf parsley, chopped,
   plus more for garnish.

Salt and freshly ground black pepper.

1 tablespoon extra virgin olive oil.

METHOD

1. Preheat oven to 200 degrees Celsius. In a large pot of boiling salted water cook spaghetti 2 minutes shy of package directions as they will continue to cook in the oven. Drain and rinse under cold water.

2. In a large bowl, toss cooled spaghetti with 2 beaten eggs, shredded mozzarella, ½ cup grated parmesan cheese and 1 cup of marinara sauce. Spray a muffin tin with cooking spray and nest spaghetti inside and using tongs give them a twirl. Using the bottom of a very small glass, press firmly down to create a well.

3. Bake until set, 15 minutes and if they puff up while baking press down again with the glass.

4. While spaghetti cups bake, make meatballs-

5. In a large bowl, combine minced beef, bread crumbs, garlic, remaining egg, remaining ¼ cup parmesan and parsley. Season with salt and pepper. Make sure it's all combined well and roll into small balls. Good thing about this is that you can make these in advance and freeze and use them when needed.

6. In a large skillet over medium heat, heat oil. Brown meatballs, 4 minutes per side, then drain fat. Pour over 2 cups marinara sauce and let simmer for 5 minutes.

7. Spoon meatballs onto the spaghetti nests and garnish with parmesan and parsley. Serve immediately.

Sauce

 SPAGHETTI MADNESS

Marinara Sauce

 **Prep Time 15 mins | Cook Time 30 mins**    12 people

Most of us have probably bought jarred marinara sauce at one time or another. While some brands taste superior to others, they all use similar ingredients of tomatoes, onions, garlic, sometimes sofrito, basil and other herbs. But with this homemade Marinara sauce recipe you will always enjoy superior marinara sauce. A sauce with many uses and once cooled down completely can be frozen in zip lock bags for up to 3 months.

INGREDIENTS

4 x 400g cans whole peeled tomatoes, San Marzano
   recommended but Roma tomatoes are ok.

1 and ½ cup Sofrito, (½ cup finely diced onion,
   ½ cup finely diced celery, ½ cup finely diced carrot).

1 tablespoon minced garlic.

1 teaspoon dried oregano

¼ teaspoon red chilli flakes, optional.

1 teaspoon salt

¼ teaspoon cracked black pepper.

¼ cup fresh basil, chopped.

METHOD

1. Drain the tomatoes in a colander set in a bowl. Crush tomatoes using your clean hands, breaking up into smaller chunks. Allow the tomatoes to sit and drain in the colander for 5 minutes. Reserve the tomato juice.

2. Heat a large skillet over medium heat. Once hot, add the olive oil. When the oil starts to shimmer add the sofrito and sauté until they are softened and lightly browned, about 5 minutes.

3. Add the garlic, oregano, chilli flakes, salt and pepper, stir and cook until fragrant, around 30-40 seconds. Add the strained tomatoes and stir to combine. Increase heat to medium to high, cook and stir frequently, until the liquid evaporates and the sauce begins to brown in the edges of the pan, about 10 minutes.

4. Add 2 and ½ cups of the reserved tomato juice, stir the sauce, scraping any browned bits from the pan. Reduce heat to a simmer, stir and cook until the sauce has thickened, about 10 minutes. Stir in the chopped basil. Taste sauce and season with more salt, pepper and chilli flakes if needed. Happy days!

Basil Pesto Sauce

 **Prep Time 15 mins | Cook Time 15 mins**    9-10 people

I absolutely adore basil pesto! All of that super fresh basil, garlic, toasted pine nuts and pecorino cheese flavour! It's something I especially start to crave more once the weather gets warm. While store bought pesto can taste great, absolutely nothing compares to the flavour of homemade!

INGREDIENTS

2 large bunches of fresh basil

4 garlic cloves, smashed and peeled.

½ cup pine nuts, lightly toasted.

1 cup extra virgin olive oil.

1 and ½ cup freshly grated pecorino romano cheese.

1 teaspoon salt, plus more for seasoning.

freshly ground black pepper.

1 teaspoon red chilli flakes, optional.

METHOD

1. Pluck large basil leaves from stems, the smaller ones are ok and you should have about 4-5 cups of leaves. Wash the basil leaves in a large bowl of cold water and dry in a salad spinner or pat dry with paper towels.

2. Put the basil, garlic and pine nuts in a food processor and pulse until coarsely chopped. With the processor running, gradually add the olive oil and process until the pesto is smooth. Transfer the pesto to a large bowl and stir in ½ cup of the cheese. Season with salt and pepper. This perfect for freezing. When frozen I just use an ice cream scoop for whatever I need at that time. And here is a real life hack, fill up ice cube trays with the pesto and freeze…brilliant!

Cream Cheese Alfredo Sauce

 **Prep Time 5 mins** | **Cook Time 10 mins**    10 people

Alfredo sauce with cream cheese is an easy 30 minute dinner that is so creamy delicious and full of flavour. Serve over your favourite pasta for a delicious dinner that will be another family favourite. You only need a few simple ingredients to make something spectacular. Buon appetito.

INGREDIENTS

½ cup salted butter.

225g cream cheese, cut into chunks.

1 and ½ teaspoons garlic powder.

1 cup heavy whipping cream.

1 cup chicken broth or stock.

225g freshly grated parmesan cheese.

½ teaspoon salt, or less to taste.

¼ teaspoon ground black pepper.

METHOD

1. Melt butter in a skillet or a saucepan with high sides over medium to high heat. Once melted, add in the chunks of cream cheese and garlic powder. Stir with a whisk until mostly smooth and mixed together. This will take a couple of minutes, at this stage it may look curdled and not perfectly smooth but that's fine, it'll smooth out when the liquid is added.

2. Now, add the whipping cream and chicken broth a bit at a time, while whisking constantly. Bring to a low boil. Once boiling, reduce heat to medium-low and add the parmesan cheese, salt and pepper. Let simmer for 5-10 minutes until slightly thickened, stirring occasionally.

3. Take the pan off the heat and let it sit for about 5 minutes so it can thicken up.

4. Note - the Alfredo sauce won't thicken up all the way until you turn off the heat and let the Alfredo sauce sit there for several minutes. Be sure to allow about 5 minutes to let the sauce sit and rest before serving with your favourite pasta,

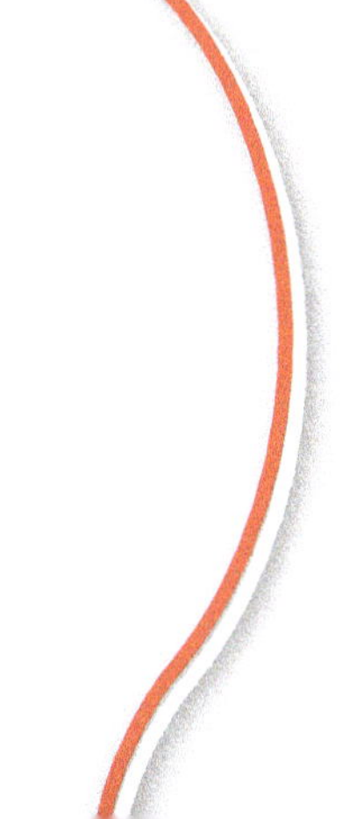

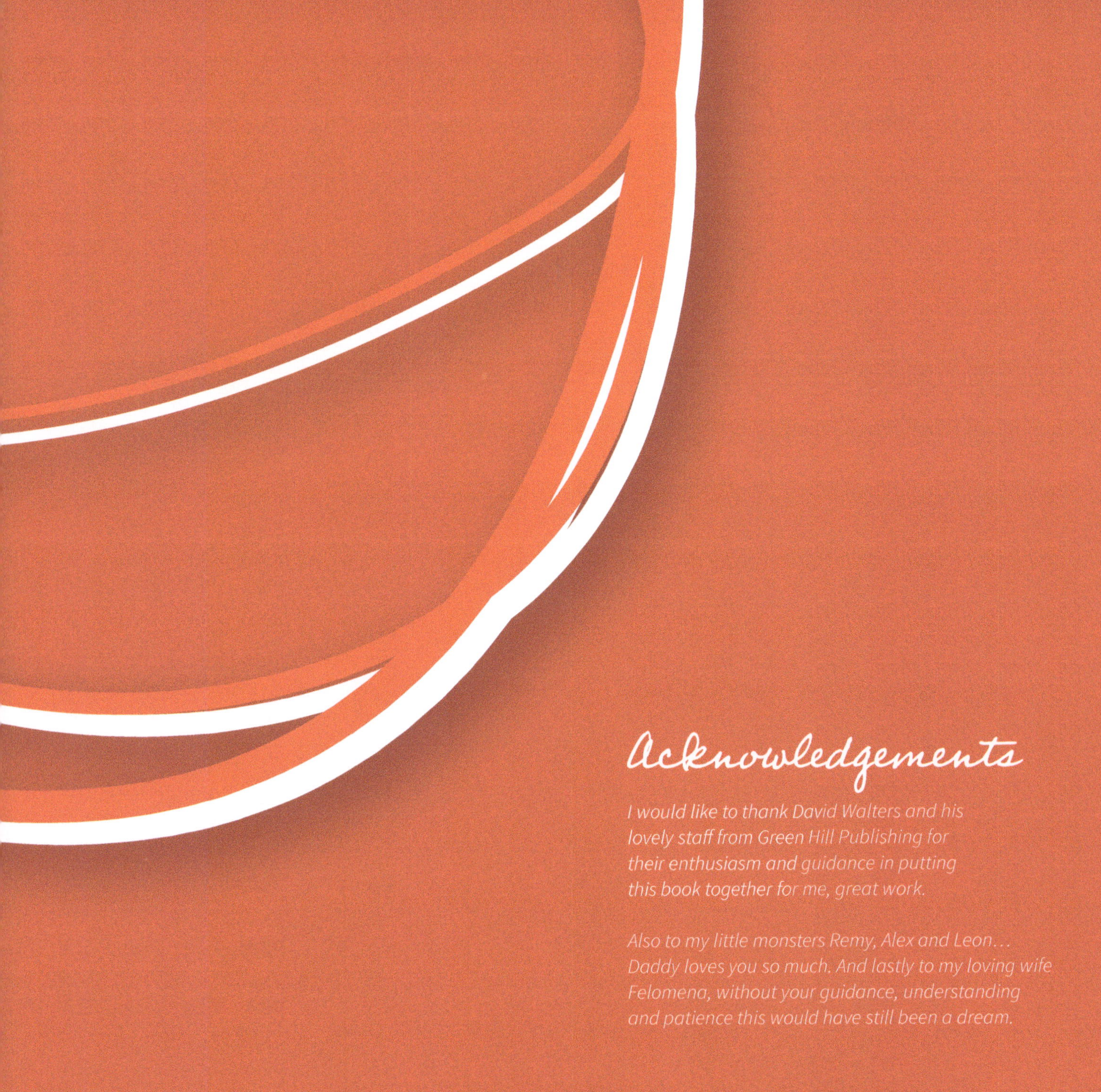

Acknowledgements

I would like to thank David Walters and his lovely staff from Green Hill Publishing for their enthusiasm and guidance in putting this book together for me, great work.

Also to my little monsters Remy, Alex and Leon… Daddy loves you so much. And lastly to my loving wife Felomena, without your guidance, understanding and patience this would have still been a dream.

Conversion Chart

WEIGHT

¼ oz	8 g		10 oz	315 g
½ oz	15 g		11 oz	345 g
1 oz	30 g		12 oz	375 g
2 oz	60g		13 oz	410 g
3 oz	90 g		14 oz	440 g
4 oz	125 g		15 oz	470 g
5 oz	155 g		16 oz	500 g
6 oz	185 g		24 oz	750 g
7 oz	220 g		32 oz	1 kg
8 oz	250 g		48 oz	1.5 kg
9 oz	280 g		64 oz	2 kg

LIQUIDS

CUP	IMPERIAL	METRIC
¼ cup	2 fl oz	60 ml
⅓	2 ¾ fl oz	80 ml
100 ml	3 ½ fl oz	100 ml
½ cup	4 fl oz	125 ml
	5 fl oz	150 ml
¾ cup	6 fl oz	180 ml
	7 fl oz	200 ml
1 cup	8 ¾ fl oz	250 ml
1 ¼ cup	10 ½ fl oz	310 ml
1 ½ cup	13 fl oz	375 ml
1 ¾ cup	15 fl oz	430 ml
	16 fl oz	475 ml
2 cups	17 fl oz	500 ml
2 ½ cups	21 ½ fl oz	625 ml
3 cups	26 fl oz	750 ml
4 cups	35 fl oz	1L
5 cups	44 fl oz	1.25 l
6 cups	52 fl oz	1.5 l

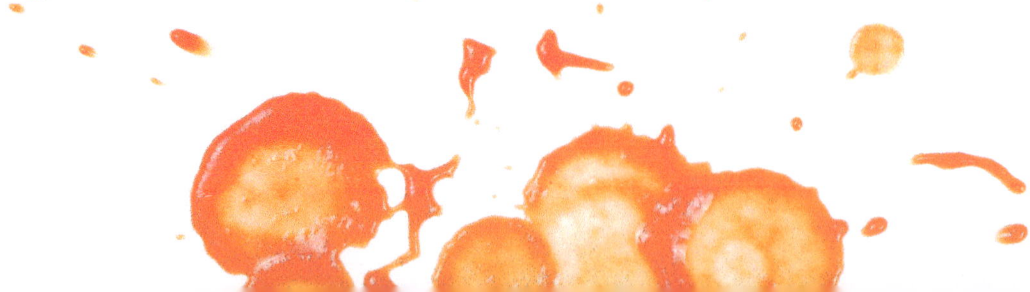

CUPS AND SPOONS

1 metric tablespoon = 20 ml

1 metric teaspoon = 5 ml

1 cup = 250 ml (8 fl oz)

TEMPERATURE CONVERSION

FAHRENHEIT (F)	ELECTRIC CELCIUS (C)	ELECTRIC FAN FORCED (C)	GAS
250	120	100	1
300	150	130	2
325	160	140	3
350	180	160	4
375	190	170	5
400	200	180	6
450	230	210	7